FREEDOM

EMBROIDERED QUILTS OF SLAVE LIFE IN THE CIVIL WAR

Lolita Newman

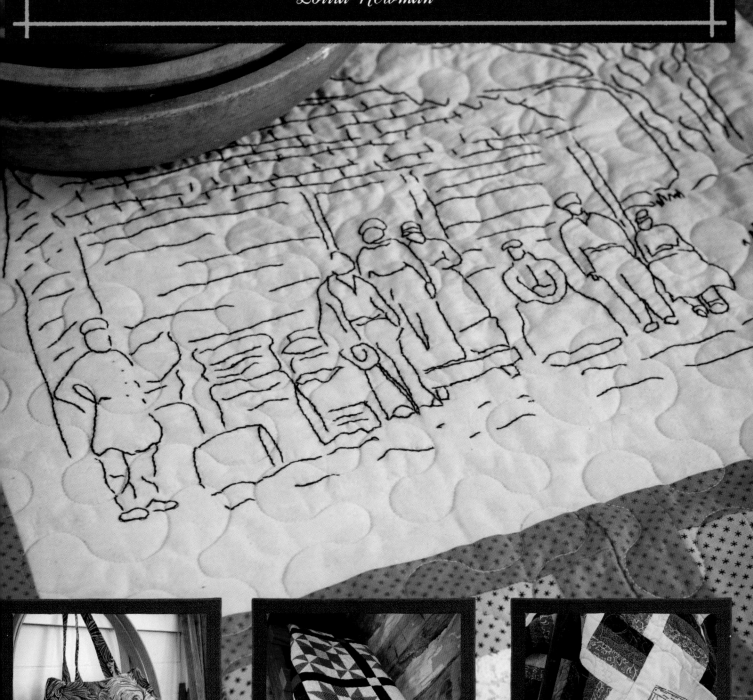

FREEDOM GONE
EMBROIDERED QUILTS OF SLAVE LIFE IN THE CIVIL WAR
By Lolita Newman

Editor: Judy Pearlstein
Designer: Bob Deck
Photography: Aaron T. Leimkuehler
Illustration: Eric Sears
Technical Editor: Nan Doljac
Photo Editor: Jo Ann Groves

Location photos were shot at Shoal Creek Living History Museum,
Kansas City, Missouri.

Published by:
Kansas City Star Books
1729 Grand Blvd.
Kansas City, Missouri, USA 64108

First edition, first printing
ISBN: 1-61169-096-5

Library of Congress Control Number: 2013940640

Printed in the United States of America by Walsworth Publishing Co., Marceline, MO

To order copies, call StarInfo at (816) 234-4242.

KANSAS CITY STAR
QUILTS
Continuing the Tradition

PickleDish.com
The Quilter's Home Page

TABLE OF CONTENTS

ABOUT THE AUTHOR

Give her of the fruit of her hands; and let her own works praise her in the gates.

Proverbs: 31:31

During her family ancestral search to find her own connection with slavery, Lolita was moved to create an heirloom that links her past to the present. After many coversations with a friend, her pattern line was born. She started Stitchin' by the River Studio, a nod to her Cane River, Louisiana, roots. She has been sewing for more than 20 years. For eleven of those years, she has been quilting and teaching. Lolita is a self-taught quilter and embroiderer. She lives in southern California with her husband and two children. She also finds time to knit, crochet and bake.

Find more of her work on **www.stitchinbytheriver. blogspot.com** and **www.stitchinbytheriver.com**. "Living in the present, stitchin' the past, for our future."

WORKDAY

Picking cotton may have been the main chore on the plantation. But they did everything: laundry, cooking, cleaning, and tending to the chickens. This quilt depicts some of those chores.

Finished Quilt 44" x 55 ¼"

Fabric Requirements

- Black fabric, ½ yard
- Tea dyed fabric, ⅔ yard
- Beige fabric, ⅝ yard
- Red fabric, 1 ½ yards
- Orange fabric, ⅝ yard
- Backing fabric, 3 yards
- Binding fabric, ⅜ yard
- Black embroidery floss, 4 skeins

TEMPLATES ARE ON PAGES 68-73

For Stitchery

Cut stitchery background from tea dyed muslin. Cut two 11" x width of fabric. Cut six 11" squares. *I double my fabric because I carry my stitches and the black floss may show through the fabric. You may or may not want or need to double your muslin due to the thickness of the fabric. These blocks will be set on point, so be sure to trace the designs onto the fabric on point, as shown in the diagram on page 12.*

Cutting

All strips are cut across the width of the fabric unless noted otherwise. While cutting, be sure to label your pieces for ease in assembling the two blocks.

- ❖ Cut down completed stitcheries to 8 ½" square, being careful to center your design on the fabric so your stitching won't be lost in the seam allowance.

Beige fabric:

- ❖ Cut one 3 ⅜" strip (4" x 9" block).
  - ◆ Sub-cut six 3 ⅜" squares.
- ❖ Cut three 2 ⅞" strips (both blocks).
  - ◆ Sub-cut 36 – 2 ⅞" squares. Separate 12 squares in one stack (4" x 9" block corner triangles) and 24 in another stack (9-patch diamond blocks). Cut once on the diagonal for all squares.
- ❖ Cut one 5 ¼" strip. Cut strip into six 5 ¼" squares. Cut each square two times on the diagonal to yield 24 setting triangles, four for each block (4" x 9" block side triangles).

Black fabric:

- ❖ Cut one 1 ½" strip (4" x 9" block).
- ❖ Cut one 2 ⅜" strip (9-patch diamond).
- ❖ Cut five 2 ½" strips (1st border).

Orange fabric:

- ❖ Cut two 2 ½" strips (9-patch diamond).
  - ◆ Sub-cut 24 - 2 ½" squares.
- ❖ Cut three 2 ⅜" strips (9-patch diamond).
- ❖ Cut four 1 ½" strips (4" x 9" block).

Red fabric:

- ❖ Cut two 2 ⅜" strips (9-patch diamond).
- ❖ Cut four 1 ½" strips (4" x 9" blocks).
- ❖ Cut two 6 ⅝" squares. Cut each square once on the diagonal (four corner triangles of quilt).
- ❖ Cut one 12 ⅝" strip. Sub-cut into three 12 ⅝" squares. Cut each square twice on the diagonal (ten setting triangles).
- ❖ Cut six 3 ½" strips (2nd border).

Backing:

- ❖ Cut backing in half, 1 ½ yards each. Sew together along the long side after cutting off selvage.

Binding:

- ❖ Cut six 2 ¼" strips. Sew end to end for continuous straight binding.

BLOCK ONE - *9-Patch Diamond*

FINISHED BLOCK 8"

Unit 1

❖ Sew together the two red, 2 ⅜" strips and one orange, 2 ⅜" in the following order: red, orange, red. Press towards the red fabric. Cut 12 – 2 ⅜" segments. Set aside.

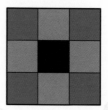

Unit 2

❖ Sew together two orange, 2 ⅜" strips and one black, 2 ⅜" strip: orange, black, orange. Press towards the black fabric. Cut six 2 ⅜" segments.

❖ Sew together two unit 1s and one unit 2 to make a 9-patch square. Repeat to make a total of six. Press well. Set aside.

❖ Sew together one orange square and two beige triangles. Press towards the orange fabric. Repeat to make a total of 24 units.

❖ Refer to block diagram and sew together six nine-patch diamond blocks. Press well, set aside.

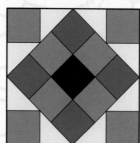

BLOCK TWO - *4" x 9" block*

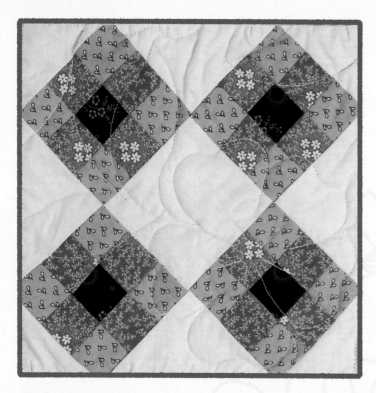

FINISHED BLOCK 8"

Unit 1

❖ Sew together two orange, 1 ½" strips and one red, 1 ½" strip: orange, red, orange. Press towards the orange fabric. Repeat for a total of two strips. Cut 48 – 1 ½" segments. Set aside.

Unit 2

❖ Sew together two red, 1 ½" strips and one black, 1 ½" strip: red, black, red. Press towards the black fabric. Cut 24 – 1 ½" segments.

❖ Sew together two unit 1s and one unit 2 to make a total of 24 – 9-Patch blocks.

❖ To make the 4" x 9" block, use four 9-Patch blocks, one 3 ⅜" beige square, four beige side triangles and four beige corner triangles. Use the diagram to complete the block. Press well. Repeat for a total of six 4" x 9" blocks.

Top Assembly

Use the quilt assembly diagram on page 12 to assemble the quilt.

Layer, quilt and bind.

ASSEMBLY DIAGRAM

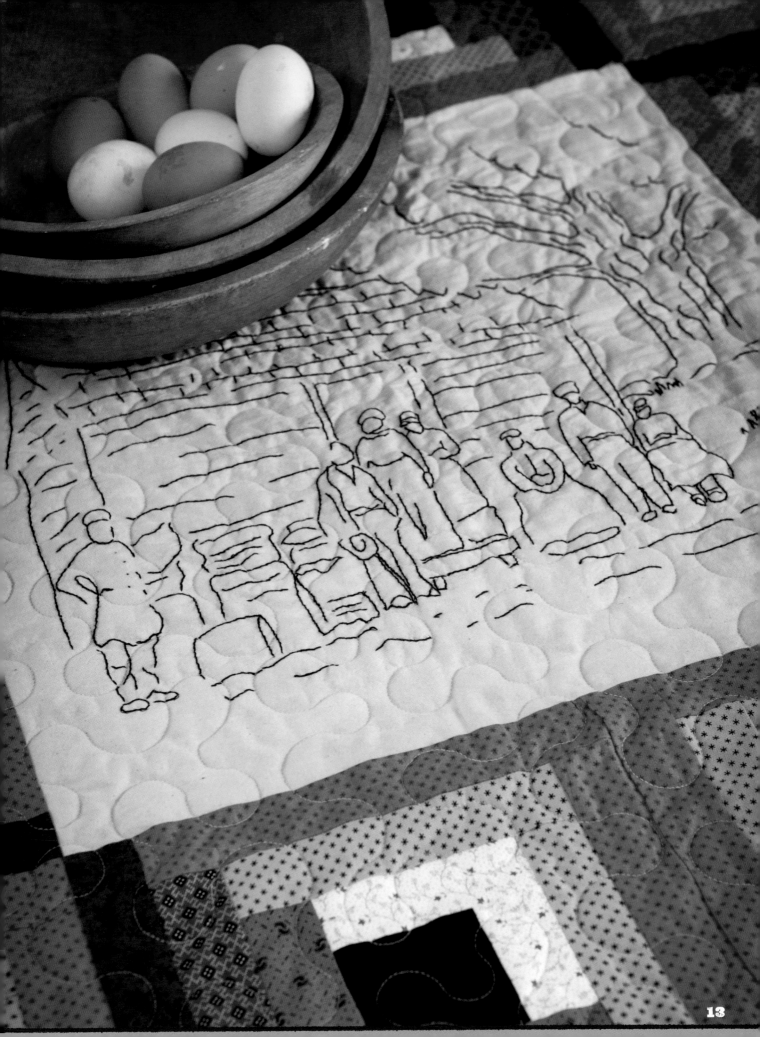

FAMILY IS...

Being sold from one plantation to another and separated from your birth family was a harsh reality. Bonding with those you were now to live and work with was a necessity, creating new families during your lifetime.

Finished Quilt 52" x 52"

Fabric Requirements

- Dark green fabric, ⅜ yard
- Medium green fabric, ⅜ yard
- Light green fabric, ¼ yard
- Light beige fabric, ¼ yard
- Medium beige fabric, ¼ yard
- Orange fabric, ⅜ yard
- Tea dyed muslin, ¾ yard
- Black fabric, 1 ½ yards
- Backing fabric, 3 ⅓ yards
- Black embroidery floss, 3 skeins

For Stitchery

Cut background from tea dyed muslin 24" square. *I double my fabric because I carry my stitches and the black floss may show through the fabric. You may or may not want or need to double your muslin due to the thickness of the fabric.*

Cutting

All strips are cut across the width of the fabric unless noted otherwise.

❖ Cut down completed stitchery to 20 ½" square, being careful to center your design on the fabric so your stitching won't be lost in the seam allowance.

Black fabric:

❖ Cut one 3" strip.

   ◆ Sub-cut 12 – 3" squares.

❖ Cut five 6 ½" strips (border).

❖ Cut six 2 ¼" strips (binding).

Light beige:

❖ Cut three 1 ¾" strips.

   ◆ From one strip, cut 12 – 1 ¾" x 3" rectangles.
   ◆ From the last two strips, cut 12 – 1 ¾" x 4 ¼" rectangles.

TEMPLATES ARE ON PAGES 74-77

Medium beige:

❖ Cut four 1 ¾" strips.

   ◆ From two strips, cut 12 – 1 ¾" x 5 ½" rectangles.
   ◆ From the last two strips, cut 12 – 1 ¾" x 6 ¾" rectangles.

Orange:

❖ Cut six 1 ¾" strips.

   ◆ From three strips, cut 12 – 1 ¾" x 8" rectangles.
   ◆ From the last three strips, cut 12 – 1 ¾" x 9 ¼" rectangles.

Light green:

❖ Cut four 1 ¾" strips.

   ◆ From two strips, cut 12 – 1 ¾" x 4 ¼" rectangles.
   ◆ From the last two strips, cut 12 – 1 ¾" x 5 ½" rectangles.

Medium green:

❖ Cut five 1 ¾" strips.

   ◆ From two strips, cut 12 – 1 ¾" x 6 ¾" rectangles.
   ◆ From the last three strips, cut 12 – 1 ¾" x 8" rectangles.

Dark green:

❖ Cut six 1 ¾" strips.

   ◆ From three strips, cut 12 – 1 ¾" x 10 ½" rectangles.
   ◆ From the last three strips, cut 12 – 1 ¾" x 9 ¼" rectangles.

Backing:

❖ Cut backing fabric into two 1 ⅔ yard pieces. Sew together two long sides of the fabric. Press the seam open.

Block Assembly

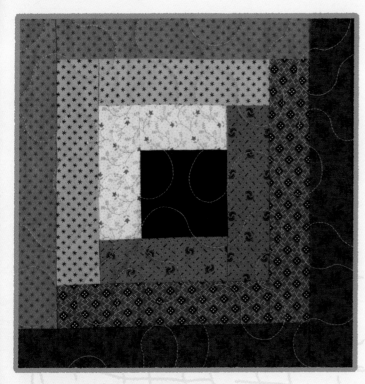

FINISHED BLOCK 10"

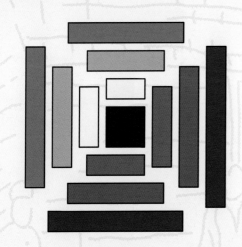

Sew piece 2 to piece 1. Sew piece 3 to the one-two unit.
Sew each additional piece in order to the previous unit.

1. 3" square black

2. 1 ¾" x 3" light beige

3. 1 ¾" x 4 ¼" light beige

4. 1 ¾" x 4 ¼" light green

5. 1 ¾" x 5 ½" light green

6. 1 ¾" x 5 ½" medium beige

7. 1 ¾" x 6 ¾" medium beige

8. 1 ¾" x 6 ¾" medium green

9. 1 ¾" x 8" medium green

10. 1 ¾" x 8" orange

11. 1 ¾" x 9 ¼" orange

12. 1 ¾" x 9 ¼" dark green

13. 1 ¾" x 10 ½" dark green

Repeat to make 12 blocks.

Top Assembly

Use the quilt assembly diagram on page 18 to assemble the quilt.

Layer, quilt and bind.

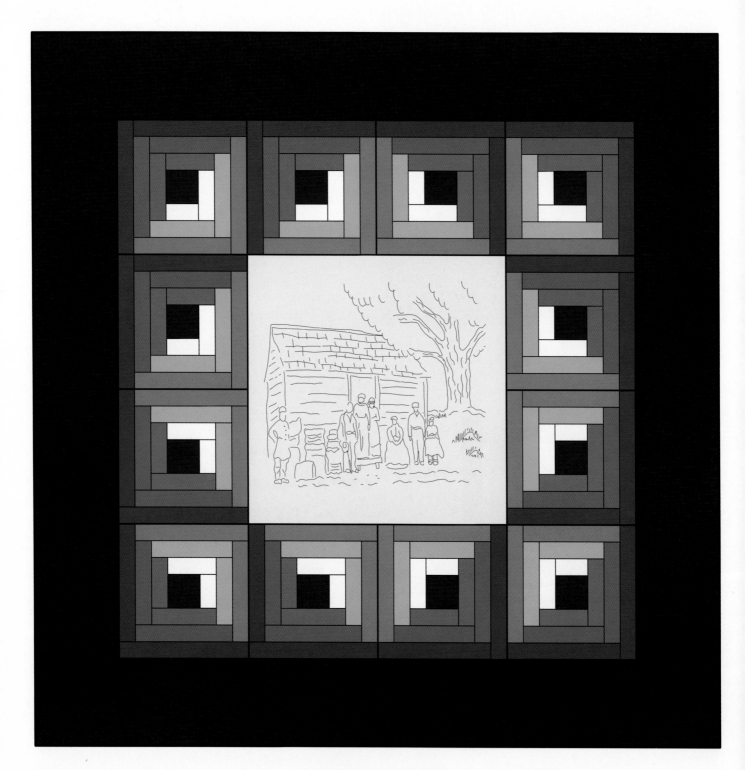

ASSEMBLY DIAGRAM

SLAVE QUARTERS

Slave quarters were fairly rough, to say the least, compared to the main house. Not all were lucky enough to have chimneys either. Back then, that was a luxury.

Finished Quilt 57" x 49"

Fabric Requirements

- Olive Green, ⅝ yard
- Purple, ⅞ yard
- Beige print, 1 ⅛ yards
- Tea dyed fabric, 1 yard
- Black, ⅞ yard
- Backing, 3 yards
- Black embroidery floss, 3 skeins

TEMPLATES ARE ON PAGES 78-83

For Stitchery

Cut background from tea dyed muslin, 36" x 22".
I double my fabric because I carry my stitches and the black floss may show through the fabric. You may or may not want or need to double your muslin depending on the thickness of the fabric.

Cutting

All strips are cut across the width of the fabric unless noted otherwise.

❖ Cut down completed stitchery to 27 ½" x 19 ½", being careful to center your design on the fabric so your stitching won't be lost in the seam allowance.

From purple fabric:

❖ Cut five strips, 1 ⅝" (chain).

❖ Cut five 4 ½"strips (1st border).

From beige fabric:

❖ Cut two 1 ⅝" strips (chain).

  ◆ Sub-cut 28 – 1 ⅝" x 2 ¾" rectangles.

❖ Cut two 2 ¾" strips (chain).

❖ Cut four 5" strips (chain).

  ◆ Sub-cut 56 – 2 ¾" x 5" wide rectangles.

❖ Cut six 1 ⅝" strips (chain).

From olive green fabric:

❖ Cut seven 1 ⅝" strips (chain).

❖ Cut three 2 ½" strips (2nd border).

From black fabric:

❖ Cut two 1 ⅝" strips (chain).

❖ Cut seven 2 ½" strips (3rd border).

❖ Cut three 1 ½" strips (flange).

❖ Cut six 2 ¼" strips (binding).

Backing:

❖ Cut backing in half, 1 1/2 yards each. Sew together along the long side after cutting off selvage.

FINISHED BLOCK 9"

CHAIN BLOCK

Unit A

Sew together one black 1 ⅝" strip and one 1 ⅝" green strip. Press towards the dark fabric. Repeat for a total of two strips. Cut 28 – 1 ⅝" segments. Sew together two segments to make a 4-patch unit. Repeat to make a total of 14 – 4-patch units. Set aside.

Unit B

Using the 1 ⅝" green, purple and beige strips, sew together one beige strip to each of the green and purple strips, for a total of three green/beige strips, repeat for a total of three green/beige and three purple/beige strips. Press well towards the dark fabric. Cut 1 ⅝" segments for a total of 56 green and 56 purple segments. Sew together

two green segments to make a 4-patch. Continue in this manner with both the green segments and purple segments, for a total of 28 green/beige 4-patch and 28 purple/beige 4-patch. Press well and set aside.

Unit C

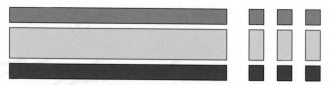

Sew together one 2 ¾" beige strip and one green 1 ⅝" strip. Press towards the dark fabric. Sew one purple strip to the opposite side of the beige strip and press towards the dark fabric. Repeat again for a total of two strip sets. Cut a total of 28 segments. Set aside.

Assemble the block as follows:
Use diagram below to assemble 14 blocks. Be sure to pay attention to color placement when assembling this block.

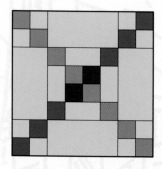

Sew one beige, 2 ¾" rectangle to a black/green 4-patch (unit A). Sew another rectangle to the opposite side. Press towards the dark fabric. Sew one unit C to the right side of the block. Then sew one unit C to the left side of the block. Press well. Sew a 2 ¾" x 5" beige rectangle to the top and bottom of this center section. Sew a green 4-patch and a purple 4-patch to the ends of a 2 ¾"x 5" beige strip. Sew to both sides of the center section. Press well. Repeat to make a total of 14 blocks.

Flange

Fold the three black, 1 ½" strips, wrong sides together and press. Baste to all four sides of the stitchery, using a ⅛" seam. Press towards the stitchery.

Top Assembly

Use the quilt assembly diagram below to assemble the quilt.

Layer, quilt and bind.

ASSEMBLY DIAGRAM

THE GARDEN BEHIND MY QUARTERS

Some slaves had better perks than others. Some were allowed to have their own garden near their quarters to help supplement their food.

Finished Quilt 67 ⅜" x 67 ⅜"

Fabric Requirements

- Cream print, 2 yards
- Burgundy print, ½ yard
- Dark green print, ⅜ yard
- Black solid, 1 ½ yards
- Light green print, 1 ⅛ yards
- Pink print, ⅜ yard
- Yellow print, ⅛ yard
- Backing fabric, 4 ¼ yards
- Binding fabric, ⅝ yard

TEMPLATES ARE ON PAGES 84-85

Cutting

All strips are cut across the width of the fabric unless noted otherwise. While cutting, be sure to label your pieces for ease in assembling the two blocks.

Light green fabric:

❖ Cut six 2 ⅞" strips (A). From three, cut 36 – 2 ⅞" squares (B).

❖ Cut seven 2 ½" strips (1ˢᵗ border).

Yellow fabric:

❖ Cut four 2 ⅞" yellow squares (H).

Cream print fabric:

❖ Cut five 2 ⅞" strips (A). From three, cut 36 – 2 ⅞" squares (C) (for corner squares 9-Patch star).

❖ Cut six 3 ¼" strips. From strips, cut 68 – 3 ¼" squares (D) (36 for half-square triangles 9-Patch star and 32 for half-square triangles Grandma's Favorite).

❖ Cut one 4" strip. From strips, cut two 4" squares.

  ♦ Cut both squares twice on the diagonal (I) (cornerstones).
  ♦ From the same strip, cut six 2 ½" squares (cornerstones).

Setting/corner triangles:

Using the same cream fabric from above:
❖ Cut two 9 ¼" strips. From these strips, use template "A" to cut eight side setting triangles.

❖ Cut one 6 ⅝" strip. From this strip, use template "B" to cut four corner triangles.

Burgundy fabric:

❖ Cut one 4" strip.

  ♦ From this, cut two 4" squares. Cut both squares twice on the diagonal (I) (cornerstones).
  ♦ From the same strip, cut six 2 ½" squares (cornerstones).

❖ Cut three 2 ⅞" strips (A). From one strip, cut nine 2 ⅞" squares (E) (center of 9-Patch star).

❖ Cut one strip, 2 ½". From this strip, cut six 2 ½" squares (J) (cornerstones).

Pink fabric:

❖ Cut three 3 ¼" strips. From strips, cut 36 – 3 ¼" squares (D) (half-square triangles 9-Patch star).

Dark green fabric:

❖ Cut three 3 ¼" strips. From strips, cut 32 – 3 ¼" squares (D).

Black fabric:

❖ Cut 19 – 2 ½" strips (seven for 2ⁿᵈ border).

  ♦ From twelve strips, cut 36 – 2 ½" x 12 ½" strips (sashing).

Backing:

❖ Cut backing in half, 2 ⅛ yards each. Sew together along the long side after cutting off selvage. Press seam open.

Binding:

❖ Cut eight 2 ¼" strips. Sew end to end.

FINISHED BLOCK 12"

NINE-PATCH STAR

❖ Sew one light green (A) and one cream (A), 2 ⅞" strips. Press towards the dark fabric. Repeat to make three total strip sets. Cut 36 – 2 ⅞" segments. Set aside.

❖ Layer 36 – 3 ¼" (D) cream squares with 36 – 3 ¼"(D) pink squares. Draw one diagonal line on the back of the light fabrics. Sew ¼" away on both sides of the drawn line. Cut on the line. Press toward the dark fabric. Repeat for a total of 72 half-square triangles. Using the diagram, sew the 2 ⅞" cream squares (C), the green/cream segments, half-square triangles, the 2 ⅞" squares (B), and the 2 ⅞" burgundy square (E); sew together the 9-Patch star block. Repeat for a total of nine blocks.

FINISHED BLOCK 12"

GRANDMA'S FAVORITE

❖ Sew together one cream, 2 ⅞" strip and one burgundy, 2 ⅞".
Press towards the dark fabric. Cut 16 – 2 ⅞" segments.

❖ Layer 32 – 3 ¼" (D) cream squares with 32 – 3 ¼" (D) dark
green squares. Draw one diagonal line on the back of the light
fabrics. Sew ¼" away on both sides of the drawn line. Cut on
the line. Press toward the dark fabric. Repeat for a total of 36 –
half-square triangles. Using the diagram, sew together the 2 ⅞"
yellow squares, the burgundy/cream segments and half-square
triangles for a total of four Grandma's Favorite blocks.

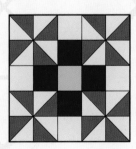

Top Assembly

Use the quilt assembly diagram on page 30 to
assemble the quilt.

Layer, quilt and bind.

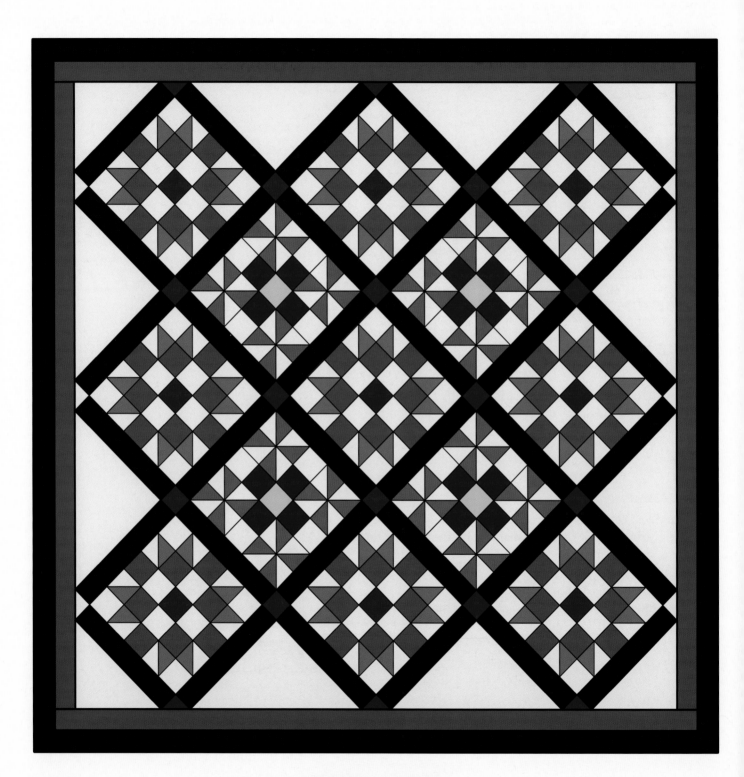

ASSEMBLY DIAGRAM

STATIONS GET READY

Homes and businesses that assisted on the Underground Railroad were called stations. These stations would feed, shelter and assist fugitive slaves on their way to freedom.

Finished Quilt 66" x 66"

Fabric Requirements

- Green print fabric, 1 ⅛ yards
- Two black print fabrics, 2 ½ yards total
- Yellow fabric, ⅛ yard
- Two white print fabrics, 1 yard total
- Red print fabric, 1 ⅛ yards
- Backing fabric, 4 ⅛ yards
- Binding fabric, ⅝ yard

TEMPLATES ARE ON PAGE 86

Cutting

All strips are cut across the width of the fabric unless noted otherwise. While cutting, be sure to label your pieces for ease in assembling the two blocks.

Black fabrics

(Use both black fabrics interchangeably as you would use in a scrappy quilt.)

- Cut eight 4 ½" strips (3rd border).

- Cut one 12 ¾" strip. From the strip, cut eight, 4 ½" x 12 ¾" wide rectangles. Use template B to cut eight roofs.

- Cut one 2 ½" strip. From the strip, cut eight, 2 ½" x 4 ½" wide rectangles (I-door).

- Cut ten 2 ⅞" strips.

Green fabric

- Cut one 12 ½" strip. From this strip, cut eight 2 ½" x 12 ½" strips (J-grass).

- Cut six 3 ½" strips (2nd border).

White fabrics

(Use both white fabrics interchangeably as you would use in a scrappy quilt.)

- Cut two 5 ¼" strips. Cut eight template A and eight template C (roof sides).

- Cut seven 2 ⅞" strips.

Yellow fabric

- Cut one 2 ½" strip. From the strip, cut eight 2 ½" squares (H).

Red fabric

- Cut one 2" strip. From the strip, cut 16 – 2 ½" x 2" squares (E).

- Cut one 5 ½" strip. From the strip, cut eight 4 ½" x 5 ½" rectangles (G).

- Cut two 2 ½" strips. From these strips, cut eight 5 ½" x 2 ½" rectangles (F).

- Cut one 12 ½" strip. Cut eight 2 ½" x 12 ½" rectangles (D).

- Cut six 2 ½" strips (1st border).

Backing

Cut the backing fabric in half lengthwise. Sew the two fabrics together along the long side.

Binding

Cut eight 2 ¼" strips. Sew end to end for continuous binding.

CHECKER BOARD

FINISHED BLOCK 12"

Unit 1

❖ Sew together three black and two white, 2 ⅞" strips in the checker board pattern. Press towards the dark fabric. Repeat for a total of two strip sets. Cut 21 – 2 ⅞" segments. Set aside.

❖ Sew together three unit 1s and two unit 2s to form a checkerboard block. Repeat for a total of five checkerboard blocks with black at the corners. Press well.

Unit 2

❖ Sew together three white and two black, 2 ⅞" strips in the checker board pattern. Press towards the dark fabric. Repeat for a total of two strip sets. Cut 19 – 2 ⅞" segments. Set aside.

❖ Sew two unit 1s and three unit 2s to form a checkerboard block with white at the corners. Repeat to make three blocks. Press well.

HOUSE BLOCK

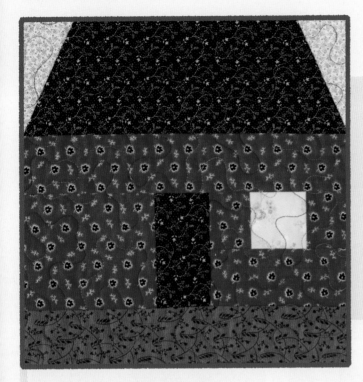

FINISHED BLOCK 12"

Unit 1

❖ Using the diagram, sew together one white (A) roof side and (C) roof side to a roof (B) strip. Press toward the dark. To the bottom of the roof, sew one 2 ½" x 12 ½" red rectangle (D). Press toward the red.

Unit 2

❖ Sew together one red, 4 ½" x 5 ½" (G) rectangle to a black 2 ½" x 4 ½" wide rectangle (I-door). Press towards the black fabric.

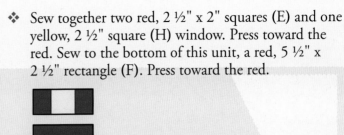

❖ Sew together two red, 2 ½" x 2" squares (E) and one yellow, 2 ½" square (H) window. Press toward the red. Sew to the bottom of this unit, a red, 5 ½" x 2 ½" rectangle (F). Press toward the red.

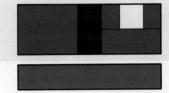

❖ Sew the **door unit** to the **window unit**. Press toward the black. Sew the green, 2 ½" x 12 ½" strips (J-grass) to the bottom of this segment.

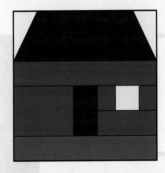

❖ Sew Unit 1 to Unit 2. Press toward Unit 1.

❖ Repeat to make eight house blocks.

Top Assembly

Using the quilt assembly diagram on page 36, sew the quilt top together.

Border strips are sewn end to end and then added to the quilt top.

Layer, quilt and bind.

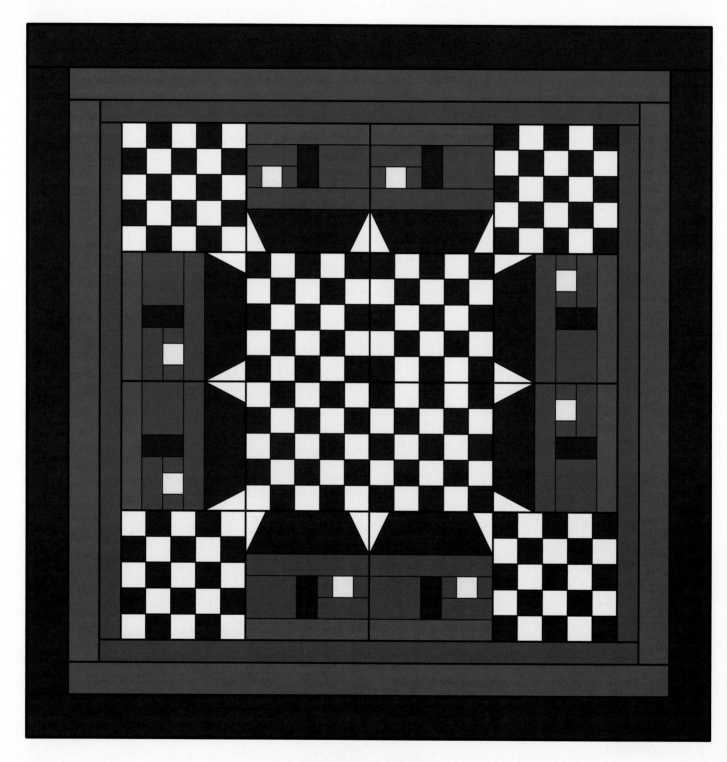

ASSEMBLY DIAGRAM

JOURNEY

When designing this quilt, I imagined the trails and wooded areas the slaves had to travel through to get to freedom. Looking at the quilt, this would be an aerial view.

Finished Quilt 76" x 86"

Fabric Requirements

- Off white, ⅝ yard
- Light green, ⅝ yard
- Medium green, 2 ⅜ yards
- Dark green, 1 yard
- Light brown, ⅝ yard
- Medium brown, 1 yard
- Dark brown, 2 ⅝ yards
- Backing fabric, 5 ¼ yards
- Binding fabric, ⅔ yard

Cutting

All strips are cut across the width of the fabric unless noted otherwise. While cutting, be sure to label your pieces for ease in assembling the two blocks.

Off white

❖ Cut 12 – 1 ⅝" strips (A).

Light green

❖ Cut three 3" strips. Cut 42 – 3" squares (E).

❖ Cut four 1 ¾" strips (F).

Medium green

❖ Cut five 4 ⅛" wide strips. From these strips, cut out 42 – 4 ⅛" squares (B).

❖ Cut three 3" wide strips. From these strips, cut 42 – 3" squares (D).

❖ Cut four 1 ¾" strips (F).

❖ Cut eight 4 ½" wide strips (2nd border).

Dark green

❖ Cut five 3 ⅞" wide strips. From these strips, cut out 42 – 3 ⅞" squares (C).

❖ Cut eight 1 ¾" strips (F).

Light brown

❖ Cut three 3" wide strips. Cut 42 – 3" squares (E).

❖ Cut four 1 ¾" strips (G).

Medium brown

❖ Cut four 4 ⅛" wide strips. From these strips, cut out 42 – 4 ⅛" squares (B).

❖ Cut four 1 ¾" strips (G).

Dark brown

❖ Cut 15 – 1 ⅝"wide strips (A).

❖ Cut three 3" wide strips. From these strips, cut 42 – 3" squares (D).

❖ Cut eight 1 ¾" strips (G).

❖ Cut eight 2 ½" wide strips (1st border).

❖ Cut nine 2 ½" wide strips (3rd border).

Backing

❖ Cut backing in half. Sew together along the long side of the fabric after cutting off selvage.

Binding fabric

❖ Cut nine 2 ¼" strips. Sew end to end for continuous binding.

Block Assembly

BLOCK ONE *Nine-Patch Block*

FINISHED BLOCK 10"

Unit 1a

❖ Using two dark brown, 1 ⅝" strips (A) and one off white, 1 ⅝" strip (A), sew together in the following order: b/w/b. Press towards the dark fabric. Repeat for a total of six strip sets.

Unit 1b

❖ Using two off white, 1 ⅝" strips (A) and one dark brown, 1 ⅝" strip (A), sew together in the following order: w/b/w. Press towards the dark fabric. Repeat for a total of three strip sets.

❖ Cut each strip set at 1 ⅝". Sew together two unit 1As and one unit 1B to make a 9-patch. Repeat for a total of sixty-three 9-patch blocks.

❖ Using the 4 ⅛" squares (B), layer right sides together, one medium green and one medium brown square. Draw a diagonal line on the back of the light green square. Sew ¼" from each side of the drawn line. Cut on the drawn line. Press towards the dark fabric. Continue to make a total of 48 half-square triangles.

❖ Using the diagram, piece together the 9-patch blocks using the half-square triangles, 9-patch blocks and dark green squares (C) for a total of 21 blocks. Press and set aside.

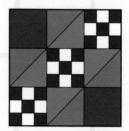

BLOCK TWO *Autumn Tints Block*

FINISHED BLOCK 10"

Green sets

❖ To make the small 4-patch blocks, sew together one 1 ¾" medium green strip (F) and one 1 ¾" dark green strip (F). Repeat for a total of four strip sets (medium/dark). Press towards the dark fabric.

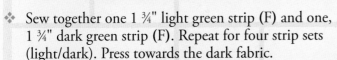

❖ Sew together one 1 ¾" light green strip (F) and one, 1 ¾" dark green strip (F). Repeat for four strip sets (light/dark). Press towards the dark fabric.

Brown sets

❖ To make the small 4-patch blocks, sew together one 1 ¾" medium brown strip (G) and one 1 ¾" dark brown strip (G). Repeat for a total of four strip sets (medium/dark). Press towards the dark fabric.

❖ Sew together one 1 ¾" light brown strip (G) and one 1 ¾" dark brown strip (G). Repeat for four strip sets (light/dark). Press towards the dark fabric.

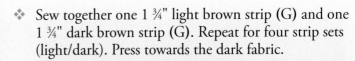

❖ Cut both the green strip sets and the brown strip sets at 1 ¾"wide. Sew together one green medium/dark 2-patch set and one green light/dark two patch set. Press. Stitch the 2-patches together to make a total of 84 green 4-patch blocks.

❖ Repeat the same process for the brown sets and make a total of 84 brown 4-patch blocks.

❖ Using the brown 4-patch, green 4-patch, light green and light brown 3" squares (E) and medium green and dark brown 3" squares (D), make the Autumn Tints block. Make a total of 21. Press well.

Top Assembly

Use the quilt assembly diagram on page 42 to assemble the quilt.

Use the quilt assembly diagram on page 42 to assemble the quilt.

Layer, quilt and bind.

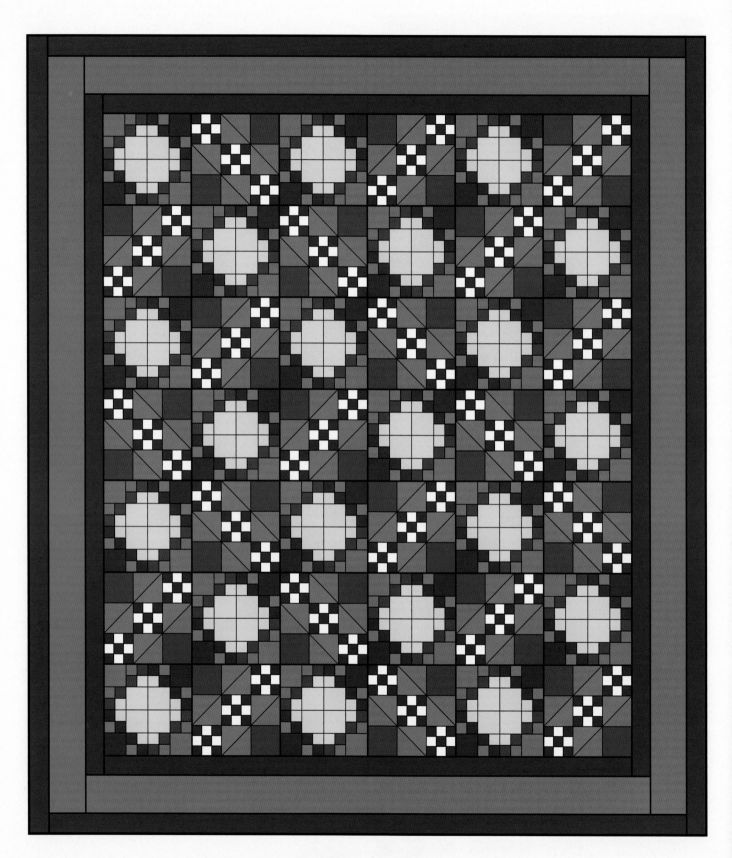

ASSEMBLY DIAGRAM

HENRY "BOX" BROWN

Henry "Box" Brown became famous for escaping slavery by mailing himself to Philadelphia in March 1849. Once free, Brown became a speaker against slavery and was forced to move to England after the passage of the Fugitive Slave Law in 1850.

Finished Quilt 45" x 45"

Fabric Requirements

- Tea dyed muslin, ⅞ yard
- Green print fabric, ½ yard
- Black print fabric, 1 yard
- Orange print fabric, ¾ yard
- Backing fabric, 3 yards
- Binding fabric, ⅜ yard
- Black embroidery floss, 2 skeins

TEMPLATES ARE ON PAGES 87-88

For Stitchery

Cut two backgrounds from tea dyed muslin 14" square. *I double my fabric because I carry my stitches and the black floss may show through the fabric. You may or may not want or need to double your muslin depending on the thickness of the fabric.*

Cutting

All strips are cut across the width of the fabric unless noted otherwise. While cutting, be sure to label your pieces for ease in assembling the two blocks.

- Cut down completed stitchery blocks to 9 ½" square, being careful to center your design on the fabric so your stitching won't be lost in the seam allowance.

From black fabric

- Cut six 1 ⅝" wide strips.
- Cut six 3 ⅞" squares.
- Cut five 3 ½" strips (2nd border).

From tea dyed muslin

- Cut six 1 ⅝" wide strips.
- Cut four 3 ⅞" squares.

From orange print

- Cut six 1 ⅝" wide strips.
- Cut two 3 ⅞" squares.

- Cut two 3 ½" squares.
- Cut four 2" strips (1st border).

From green fabric

- Cut six 1 ⅝" wide strips.
- Cut four 3 ½" squares.

Backing

- Cut backing fabric into two 1 ½ yard pieces. Sew together two long sides of the fabric after cutting off selvage. Press seam open.

Binding

- Cut five 2 ¼" strips. Sew end to end.

Henry "Box" Brown

To Philadelphia for freedom

Block Assembly

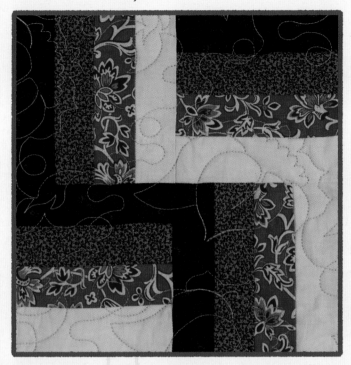

FINISHED BLOCK 9"

FINISHED BLOCK 9"

RAIL FENCE

Sew 1 ⅝" strips together, one of each color. Repeat for a total of six strip sets. Cut at 5" intervals for a total of 48 segments.

Using the diagram below, sew these segments together for a total of 12 blocks.

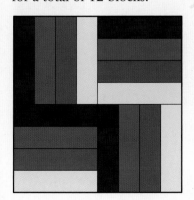

DOUBLE X BLOCK

Layer one black and one tea dyed, 3 ⅞" square. Draw a diagonal line on the back of the light fabric. Sew ¼" away on both sides of the line. Cut on the line. Press toward the dark fabric. Repeat with the other black and tea dyed, 3 ⅞" squares. Repeat with the remaining black squares and the orange 3 ⅞" squares for a total of eight black/beige half-square triangles and four black/orange half-square triangles. Using the diagram below, sew two blocks.

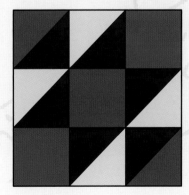

Top Assembly

Use quilt assembly diagram on page 48 to assemble quilt.

Layer, quilt and bind.

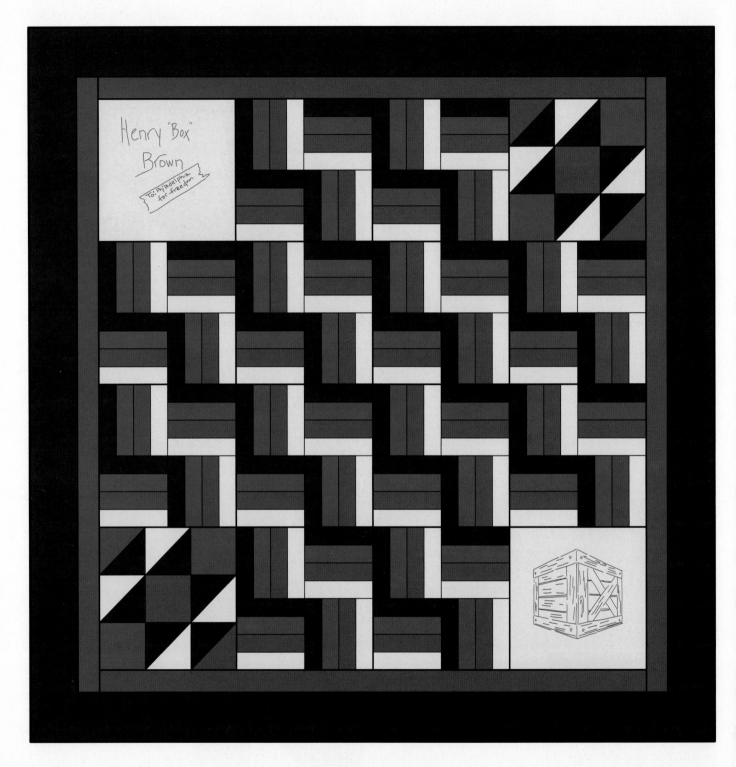

ASSEMBLY DIAGRAM

WORSHIP

Normally, Sunday was a day off and slaves were allowed to worship and go to church. Worship played a strong part in a slave's life as depicted in the hymns sung in the fields.

PREACHER Finished Quilt 23 ½" x 18 ¼"

PRAISE HOUSE Finished Quilt 18" x 15 ½"

Fabric Requirements

- ○ 1 charm pack
- ○ Tea dyed muslin, ⅔ yard
- ○ Scraps for border at least 2 ½" x 16 ½" and 2 ½" x 24 ½"
- ○ Backing fabric (enough for both), 1 yard
- ○ Binding fabric, ½ yard
- ○ Black embroidery floss, 3 skeins

TEMPLATES ARE ON PAGES 89-91

For Stitchery

Cut Praise House background from tea dyed muslin – 15" square and Preacher – 22" square. *I double my fabric because I carry my stitches and the black floss may show through the fabric. You may or may not want or need to double your muslin depending on the thickness of the fabric.*

Cutting

All strips are cut across the width of the fabric unless noted otherwise. While cutting, be sure to label your pieces for ease in assembling the two quilts.

- ❖ Cut down completed stitchery to Praise House – 12 ½" x 9 ½" and Preacher – 12 ½" x 18 ½", being careful to center your designs on the fabrics so your stitching won't be lost in the seam allowance.

Praise House

- ❖ Using the charm pack, pull seven light and seven dark fabrics. Cut a total of 14 – 4 ¼" squares.

- ❖ From four charms, cut four 3 ½" squares (corners).

Preacher

- ❖ From four charms, cut four 4 ½" squares.

- ❖ From one charm, cut one strip 2 ½" x 4 ½".

- ❖ From four charms, cut 16 – 2 ½" squares.

- ❖ Cut one 2 ½" x 4 ½" strip.

Preacher Border

- ❖ From scraps, cut one 2 ½" x 16 ½" strip (left border).

- ❖ From scraps, cut one 2 ½" x 24 ½" strip (bottom border).

Binding

- ❖ Cut three 2 ½" strips. Sew together end to end for Praise House binding.

Assembly

PRAISE HOUSE

❖ Layer one light and one dark, 4 ¼" square. Draw a diagonal line on the back of the light fabric. Sew ¼" away on both sides of the drawn line. Cut on the line. Press toward the dark fabric. Repeat for a total of 14 half-square triangles. Then, place two half-square triangle blocks together, butting up the two dark fabrics so the seam allowances nestle. Repeat the process to end with 14 quarter-square triangles.

❖ Stitch together two strips of four quarter-square triangles. Sew these to the top and the bottom of the stitchery.

❖ Stitch together two strips of three quarter-square triangles and sew one of the 3 ½" squares to each end. Add these to the sides of the Praise House unit.

❖ Layer, quilt, and bind.

PREACHER

❖ Sew two 4-patch blocks to either side of a 4 ½" square. Attach to the right side of the stitchery.

❖ For the top border, sew together the three remaining 4 ½" squares and the two 4-patch blocks, as shown in the photo on page 50, and then add the 2 ½" x 4 ½" strip, before attaching to the top of the stitchery.

❖ To the left side, add the 2 ½" x 16 ½" strip.

❖ To the bottom, add the 2 ½" x 24 ½" strip.

❖ Layer, quilt, and bind.

HENRY HOUSE HILL

This hill was an important sight for both the First and Second Battle of Bull Run. The hill was named for the occupant of the home on the hill, Dr. Isaac Henry and his family.

Finished Quilt 19 ½" x 15 ½"

Fabric Requirements

- Tea dyed muslin, ½ yard
- 1 charm pack
- Backing fabric, 1 fat quarter
- Binding fabric, ¼ yard
- Tri Recs Tool by EZ Quilting
- Black embroidery floss, 2 skeins

TEMPLATES ARE ON PAGES 92-93

For Stitchery

Cut stitchery background from tea dyed muslin 13" x 19". Cut two. *I double my fabric because I carry my stitches and the black floss may show through the fabric. You may or may not want or need to double your muslin depending on the thickness of the fabric.*

Cutting

- Cut down completed stitchery to 16 ½" x 10 ½", being careful to center your design on the fabrics so your stitching won't be lost in the seam allowance.

- Using the charm pack, select eight squares, ranging from light to dark. Cut 2 – 2 ½" x 3 ½" piano keys from each charm square to make a total of 16 piano keys.

- Using the charm pack, select eight squares ranging from light to dark. Using the Tri Recs Tool, cut 34 – 2 ½" triangles.

- From binding fabric, cut two 2 ¼" strips. Sew end to end for binding.

Assembly

- Sew eight piano keys together, light to dark. Repeat for a total of two segments. Sew one strip to the top and one to the bottom of the stitchery.

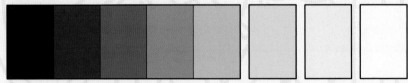

- Sew together 17 triangles, ranging from light to dark. Repeat for two segments. Sew to both sides of the stitchery. Trim ends even to stitchery.

- Layer, quilt and bind.

ASSEMBLY DIAGRAM

CARPET BAG

I would often imagine a slave receiving a carpet bag cast off from the lady of the house and using it during her daring escape north, holding what little treasures she may have. This is my version.

14" x 22 ½"

Fabric Requirements

○ Tapestry fabric, 1 ¼ yards
○ Lining fabric, 1 ¼ yards
○ Cardboard or purse support panel for bottom of bag, 5" x 21"
○ One-sided, ultra firm craft & home interfacing, 2 yards
○ 1 button
○ Leather, 6" x ⅛"

Use a ⅜" seam allowance.

TEMPLATES
ARE ON PAGES
94-95

Cutting

Tapestry fabric

❖ Cut two of the main bag on the fold.

❖ Cut two sides, 5 ½" x 15 ½".

❖ Cut two straps, 3" x 25" each.

❖ Cut one bottom, 5 ½" x 22"

Lining fabric

❖ Cut two of the main bag on the fold.

❖ Cut two sides, 5 ½" x 15 ½"

❖ Cut one bottom, 5 ½" x 22"

Assembly

❖ With right sides together, sew together both the front and back of the main bag to the side panels. Sew the bottom panel to the bag. Turn *right side* out. Repeat for the lining, leaving a 6" opening in the bottom to turn the bag later. Leave the lining wrong side out.

❖ Fold one strap, right sides together. Sew, using a ¼" seam. Repeat for the second strap. Turn both straps right side out. Press.

❖ Measure 1 ½" in from the side seams and pin the strap to the front of the main bag. Repeat for the second strap. Baste the straps to the bag.

❖ Place the main bag inside of the lining and sew around the top edge.

❖ Turn the bag right side out through the lining opening. Put in the cardboard for the bottom of the bag. Stitch lining closed.

❖ Topstitch around the top of the bag.

❖ Fold the leather in half and place on the top back of the purse. Stitch. Sew the button in place.

THE KEEPERS

We all need a little something to guard our sewing supplies. These items were created to be a little rustic with the slave in mind, who was able to make something with so little.

SEWING BOX
2" x 6"

DOLL HEAD W/CLAMP
11½"

DOLL HEAD
6"

THIMBLE COVER

DOLL HEAD PINCUSHIONS

Supplies

- Floss
- Brown fabric, 1 fat quarter
- Scraps of fabric at least 3" x 45"
- Vintage clamp
- Polyfil
- Crushed walnut shells
- Doll needle

Directions

With Clamp:

❖ Fold the fat quarter in half. Draw the doll head onto the brown fabric. Sew on the drawn line (wrong sides together). Cut out ⅛" outside the sewn line. Turn right side out. Stuff with the polyfil. Make a running stitch around the opening edge of the doll head. Insert the top of the clamp and pull tight. Run tacking stitches back and forth until secure. Wrap fabric scraps around top of doll head and base to make a scarf and shirt for the doll.

Standing Doll Head:

❖ Use the same process for the standing doll head. Stuff with both walnut shells and polyfil.

❖ Using the 3" x 45" fabric, wrap around the doll's shoulders several times and then tie a knot. Stuff the ends into the wrapped fabric. Repeat for the head of the doll.

TEMPLATE
IS ON PAGE
96

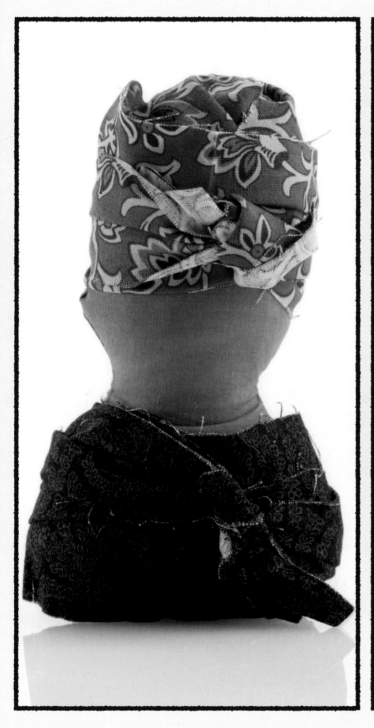

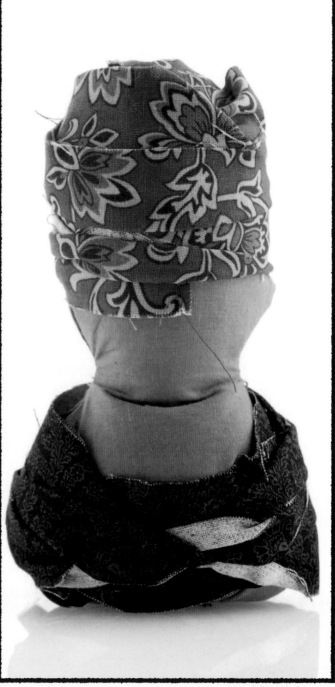

SEWING BOX

Supplies

- Scraps of wool
- Wooden box 2" x 6" (I found mine at Jo-Ann Fabric and Craft Store.)
- All purpose craft glue

TEMPLATE
IS ON PAGE
96

Directions

Cut seven hexies from the wool scraps. Glue onto the top of the stained box. Measure the inside bottom of the wood box. Cut a piece of wool to fit and glue down.

THIMBLE COVER

Supplies

O Scrap of wool
O Embroidery floss
O Safety pin (optional)

TEMPLATE
IS ON PAGE
96

Directions

Using the thimble template, cut shape from a piece of wool. Fold
so that flat edge meets the X's. (The rounded end will be the flap.)
Sew sides up with floss stopping at the X's. Use a safety pin to close
it or run four strands of floss through the flap and tie to close.

TEMPLATES

WORKDAY

WORKDAY

WORKDAY

WORKDAY

WORKDAY

FAMILY IS

Join here

Join here

FAMILY IS

Join here

Join here

SLAVE QUARTERS

SLAVE QUARTERS

Join here

Join here

Join here

SLAVE QUARTERS

Join here

Join here

SLAVE QUARTERS

Join here

Join here

SLAVE QUARTERS

Join here

Join here

Join here

SLAVE QUARTERS

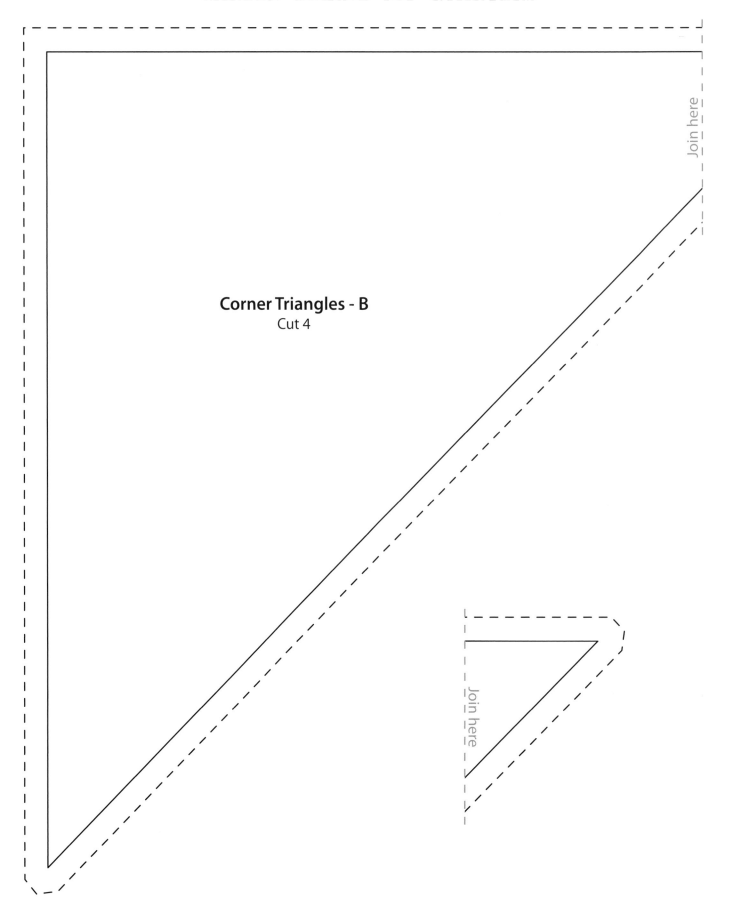

Corner Triangles - B
Cut 4

Join here

Join here

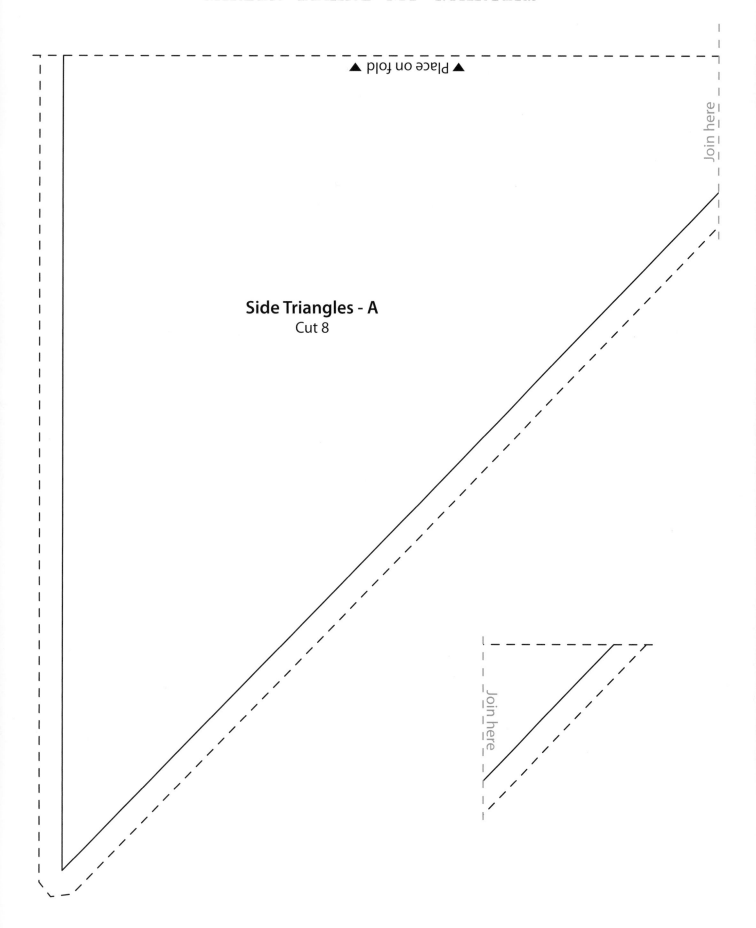

▲ Place on fold ▲

Join here

Side Triangles - A
Cut 8

Join here

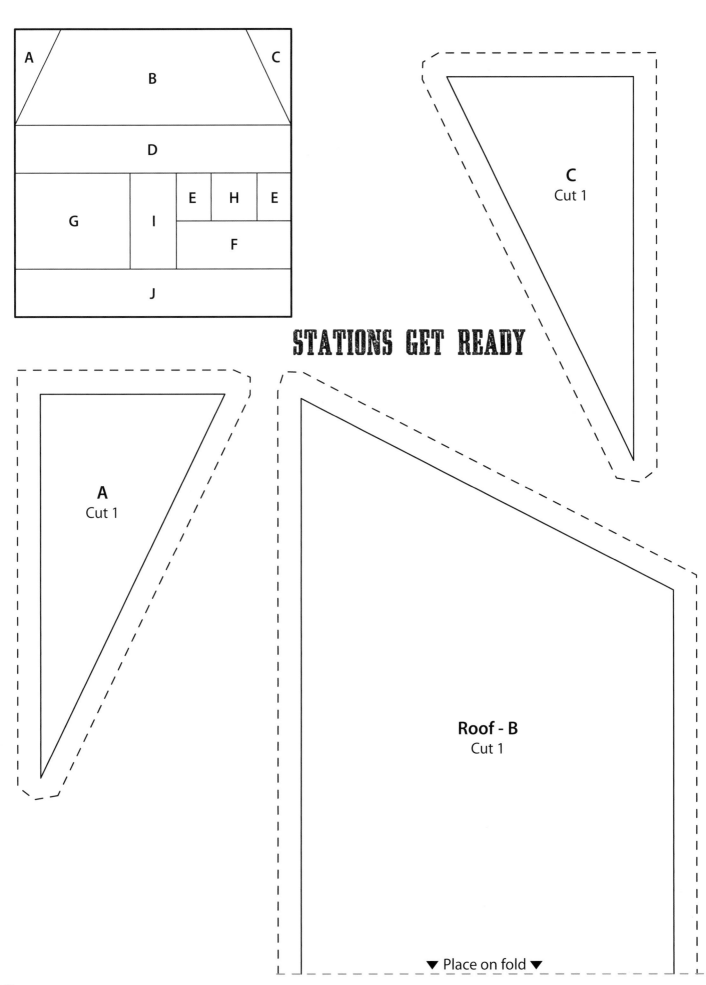

STATIONS GET READY

A
Cut 1

B
Cut 1

C
Cut 1

Roof - B
Cut 1

▼ Place on fold ▼

Henry "Box" Brown

To: Philadelphia for Freedom

HENRY "BOX" BROWN

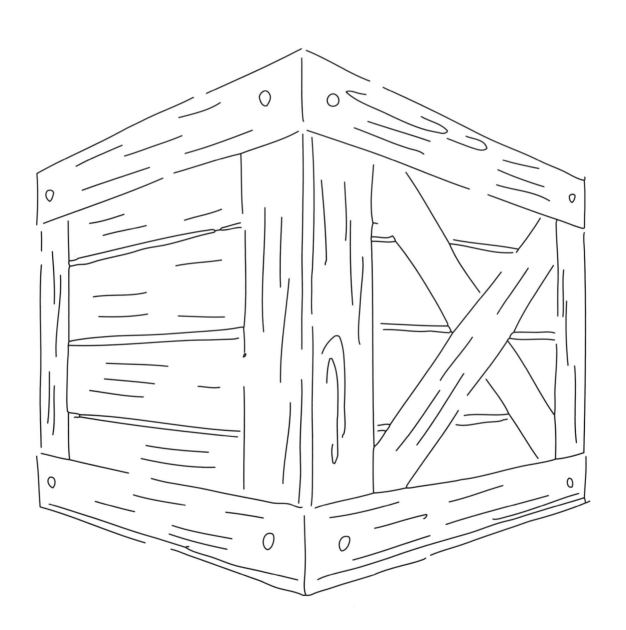

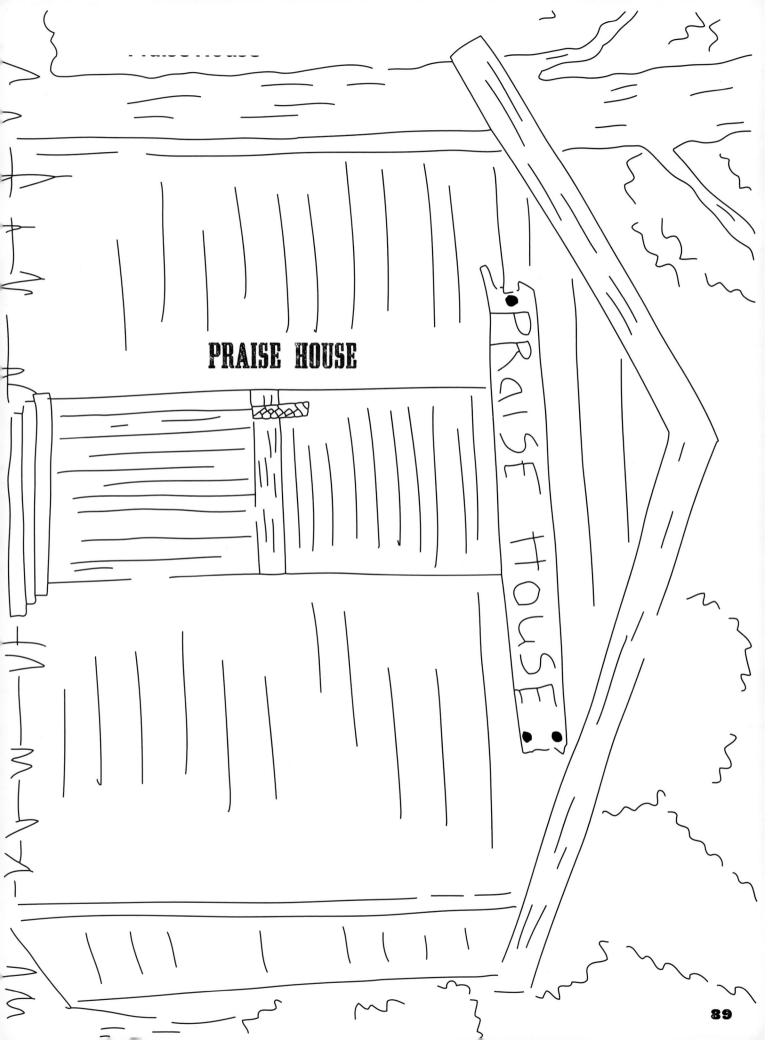

PRAISE HOUSE

Join here

PREACHER

Join here

HENRY HOUSE HILL

CARPET BAG

Main Bag
Cut 2

Join template here

Top

▼ Place on fold ▼

CARPET BAG

Bottom

Join template here

▼ Place on fold ▼

THE KEEPERS

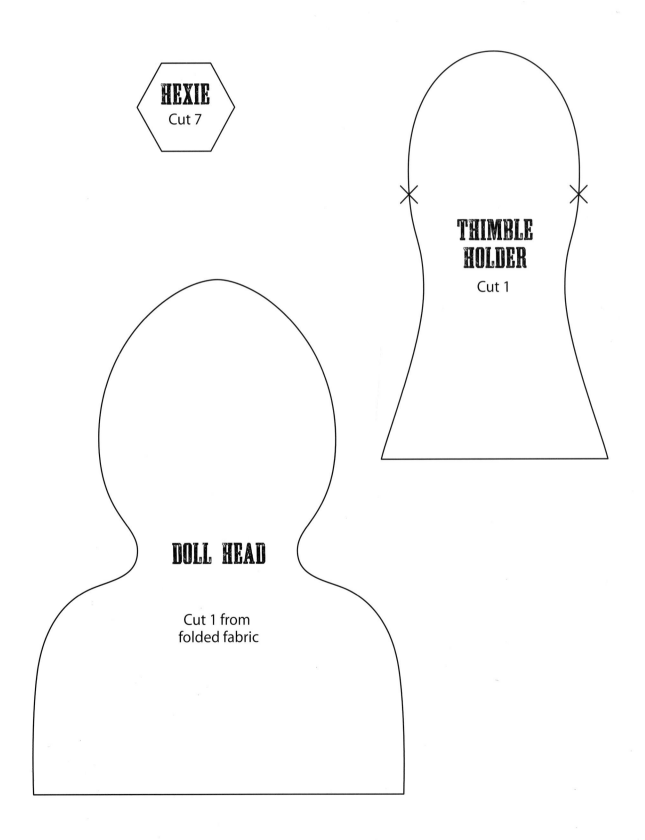

HEXIE
Cut 7

THIMBLE
HOLDER
Cut 1

DOLL HEAD

Cut 1 from
folded fabric